Hello Kitty's
How to Draw:
DRESSING PRETTY

by Carra Gamberdella   illustrated by Sachiho Hino

SCHOLASTIC INC.

New York   Toronto   London   Auckland   Sydney
Mexico City   New Delhi   Hong Kong   Buenos Aires

ISBN 0-439-67633-9

© 1976, 2004 SANRIO CO., LTD. USED UNDER LICENSE.

All rights reserved. Published by Scholastic Inc., 557 Broadway, New York, NY 10012, by arrangement with SANRIO, INC. HELLO KITTY is a registered trademark of SANRIO, INC. SCHOLASTIC and associated logos are trademarks and/or registered trademarks of Scholastic Inc.

12 11 10 9 8 7 6 5 4 3 2 1   4 5 6 7 8 9/0

Cover design by Carisa Swenson
Interior design by Bethany Dixon

Printed in China
First printing, September 2004

Hello Kitty always looks her best. Whether she's in school or at a party, Hello Kitty knows that fashion sense never goes out of style.

In this book, you'll learn how to draw Hello Kitty in her favorite outfits. There are also ideas for how to make your drawings even more spectacular. You can add jewelry and other accessories to Hello Kitty's outfit, or draw a scene around Hello Kitty. There's no limit to what you can do!

Now sharpen your pencils and turn the page.

Hello Kitty's ready to share her fashion secrets with you!

How to Draw Hello Kitty

Before you draw Hello Kitty in her fabulous outfits, you need to learn the basics of how to draw Hello Kitty!

1. Start by drawing Hello Kitty's head. Do you notice that the ear on the right is a little bigger than the ear on the left?

2. Next add Hello Kitty's eyes and nose. Isn't she cute?

3. Draw three whiskers on each of Hello Kitty's cheeks. The whiskers on the right are slightly higher than the whiskers on the left.

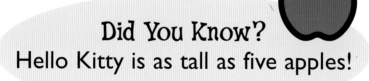

Did You Know?
Hello Kitty is as tall as five apples!

4

4. Hello Kitty loves her hair bow. Add it to her head.

Hello Kitty's hair bow is always on her left (your right). Her twin sister, Mimmy, wears a hair bow on her right (your left).

5. Now draw Hello Kitty's body. Make sure to include her collar and hem.

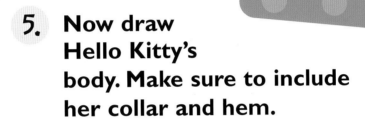

6. Finally, add Hello Kitty's arms. Don't forget to draw her sleeves.

7. Hello Kitty loves to wear a fresh flower in her hair. Try replacing her hair bow with a daisy. Now you're ready to color her in!

Back to School

Hello Kitty loves the fall—new teachers, new friends, and new school clothes! Can you draw Hello Kitty in the trendy outfit she wore on her first day of school?

1. First draw Hello Kitty's head.

2. Now add Hello Kitty's cap. Make sure to erase the lines that her cap covers.

3. The third step is to draw Hello Kitty's shirt. The bottom edge of her shirt is scalloped.

Did You Know?
Hello Kitty's favorite subjects are reading and social studies.

4. Now draw Hello Kitty's pants. There's a cargo pocket on each pant leg.

Hello Kitty knows it's best to begin your drawing with a pencil. That way, it's easy to erase. You can color your drawing later.

5. Add Hello Kitty's hands and her sneakers.

6. Finally, draw the laces on Hello Kitty's sneakers.

7. Hello Kitty loves to sparkle. Add a pretty necklace to finish her look.

Swim Team

Hello Kitty's best stroke is the butterfly. She's sure to make the team in this cute swimsuit!

1. Start by drawing Hello Kitty's head. It's tilted to her right.

2. Now add Hello Kitty's arms. Is she waving at you?

3. The next step is to draw Hello Kitty's bathing suit.

Did You Know?
Hello Kitty is also on her school's tennis team.

4. Next draw Hello Kitty's feet. Remember to erase the part of her swimsuit that is covered by her leg. She's almost ready to dive in!

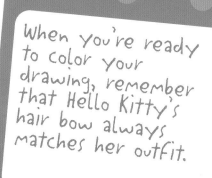

When you're ready to color your drawing, remember that Hello Kitty's hair bow always matches her outfit.

5. Add Hello Kitty's goggles. Then erase the part of the bow that is covered by her goggles.

6. Add some stars to Hello Kitty's swimsuit so she's sure to shine!

Trick or Treat?

Hello Kitty and Mimmy host a Halloween party every year. Can Hello Kitty trick her friends into thinking she's a witch?

1. Draw Hello Kitty's head and face.

2. Now add her hair bow.

3. Next draw the scary witch's hat. Don't forget to add the star!

Did You Know?
Hello Kitty has an extra-special reason to celebrate Halloween. Her birthday is the next day, November 1.

4. Every witch needs a cape. Add one to Hello Kitty's outfit. Can you draw the jack-o-lantern on the back?

Hello Kitty can't take her eyes off you! No matter which direction her body is facing, her head is always facing forward.

5. Now draw Hello Kitty's arm.

6. Finally, draw Hello Kitty's legs. You're almost ready to color her in!

7. Every witch needs a broomstick. Add one to Hello Kitty's costume so she can fly off into the night!

Go Team, Go!

Give me an *H*! Give me a *K*! Hello Kitty has lots of school spirit. Three cheers for you if you can draw Hello Kitty in her cheerleading outfit.

1. **Start by drawing Hello Kitty's head. It's tilted to her left.**

2. **Now add Hello Kitty's V-neck sweater.**

3. **Draw Hello Kitty's arms. Don't forget to add her sleeves.**

Did You Know?
Hello Kitty bakes apple pie with her mama every Thanksgiving. Yum!

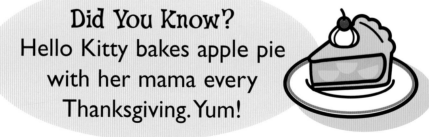

4. Next draw Hello Kitty's skirt. The folds in her skirt are called pleats.

Don't forget—the whiskers on the right are higher than the whiskers on the left.

5. Add Hello Kitty's legs. Then draw an HK on her sweater.

6. Draw a pom-pom in Hello Kitty's hand. Now that's school spirit!

7. Hello Kitty loves to cheer. Add a megaphone so everyone can hear her!

Winter Wonderland

Snow is falling and the temperature is, too! Where's Hello Kitty? She's outside in this winter wonderland. Can you draw Hello Kitty all bundled up?

1. Draw Hello Kitty's head. Her winter hat and fluffy earmuffs keep her warm.

2. Now add details to Hello Kitty's hat—draw the pom-pom and bow. Then add lines to the hat's brim.

3. Draw Hello Kitty's winter jacket.

Did You Know?
Mama designs and sews all of Hello Kitty's outfits.

4. Next draw Hello Kitty's arms. Don't forget to add her cuffs.

When you're ready to color in your drawing, use a waterproof marker. That way, the ink won't run if it gets wet.

5. Draw Hello Kitty's legs and feet. She's wearing her warmest winter boots.

6. Add a scarf around Hello Kitty's neck. She's ready to play!

7. Add a snowman to Hello Kitty's world for an even more wonderful winter scene!

Happy Holidays

On Christmas Day, Hello Kitty likes to bake cookies and play in the snow. But most of all, she loves to dress in her holiday best!

1. **Begin by drawing Hello Kitty's head and face. Then add her bow.**

2. **Next draw Hello Kitty's Santa hat.**

3. **Draw Hello Kitty's scarf so she's sure to stay nice and warm.**

Did You Know?
Mimmy is more than Hello Kitty's twin sister—she's her best friend, too!

4. Now draw Hello Kitty's arm.

Hello Kitty has a hair bow in every color of the rainbow except yellow. Only Mimmy wears a yellow bow.

5. Finish your drawing by adding her body—don't forget her tail!

6. The holiday season is for giving. Can you add the gift that Hello Kitty will give to Mimmy?

Dancing Queen

Hello Kitty's dance recital is just around the corner. Can you draw this prima ballerina in her pretty pink tutu?

1. **First draw Hello Kitty's head and face.**

2. **Add her bow. Then draw a crown of flowers for her hair. How pretty!**

3. **Next draw Hello Kitty's top.**

Did You Know?
Hello Kitty also studies tap, jazz, and ballroom dancing.

18

4. Add her arms. Hello Kitty is holding her arms to the side for balance.

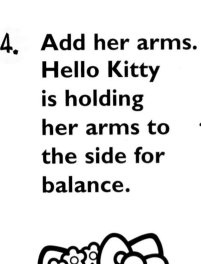

Hello Kitty knows that practice makes perfect. If you're not happy with your first drawing, just try again!

5. Draw Hello Kitty's pretty pink tutu.

6. Finally, draw Hello Kitty's feet. Make sure her ballet slippers are laced up!

7. Add some ribbons to Hello Kitty's hair for an extra-pretty look.

Party Time

Hello Kitty enjoys dressing up for her friends' birthday parties. Here's one of her favorite party outfits.

1. **Start by drawing Hello Kitty's head. Someone's winking at you!**

2. **Add her bow.**

3. **Next draw Hello Kitty's shirt and her arms.**

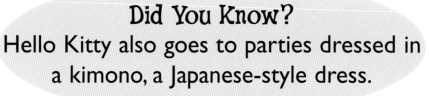

Did You Know?
Hello Kitty also goes to parties dressed in a kimono, a Japanese-style dress.

4. The next step is to add her skirt.

Remember—Hello Kitty doesn't have a mouth. Everything she says comes from her heart.

5. Now draw Hello Kitty's legs. Add her shoes, too.

6. A party outfit isn't complete without a matching purse! Add this cute bag to your drawing. Write Hello Kitty's initials on her shirt and purse. Now color her in—don't forget the polka dots!

Spring Break

The White family is vacationing on a tropical island. Grab your surfboard and join Hello Kitty as she rides the waves!

1. **Start by drawing Hello Kitty's head and face. Make sure to add a pretty flower in her hair.**

2. **Draw Hello Kitty's arm.**

3. **Do you notice that her body is facing left? Draw the outline of her body, including the leg closest to you.**

Did You Know?
Hello Kitty loves to travel, but her favorite city is her hometown of London, England.

4. Add Hello Kitty's other leg, her arm, and her tail.

Test your art skills! Try to make your drawings smaller and larger than the drawings in this book.

5. The next step is to draw Hello Kitty's bathing suit. Don't forget to add the flower!

6. Draw Hello Kitty's surfboard. It's a little taller than her.

7. Make a splash! Add a leaping dolphin to Hello Kitty's world.

Field Day

It's field day at school, and Hello Kitty is ready to race. Draw her before she runs away!

1. **Begin by drawing Hello Kitty's head. It's tilted to her left.**

2. **Draw Hello Kitty's baseball cap—remember the HK! Then erase any lines that her cap covers.**

3. **Now add Hello Kitty's sweatshirt and her arms. Don't forget to draw her sleeves!**

Did You Know?
Hello Kitty is a nickname. Kitty White is her official name.

4. The next step is to add her pants. Then draw her tail— it's peeking out from behind her hand.

When, coloring Hello Kitty's outfit, choose colors that complement each other, like red and green or yellow and purple.

5. Draw Hello Kitty's sneakers. Make sure they're laced up!

6. Add a hood and front pockets to Hello Kitty's sweatshirt.

7. Hello Kitty is made in the shade! Slip these dark sunglasses onto her for a cool look.

Spring Formal

Hello Kitty is ravishing in red. It's the end of the school year, and she's ready to make a grand entrance at her spring formal.

1. Draw Hello Kitty's head. She's wearing a special bow for this occasion!

2. Now add the top of Hello Kitty's sleeveless dress.

3. Draw Hello Kitty's arms. Don't forget her fancy white gloves!

Did You Know?
Hello Kitty's favorite accessory is her red hair bow.

4. Next draw the bottom of Hello Kitty's dress. The flower on her waist matches the flower in her bow!

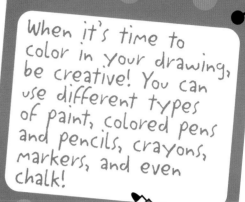

When it's time to color in your drawing, be creative! You can use different types of paint, colored pens and pencils, crayons, markers, and even chalk!

5. Draw Hello Kitty's black heels. She's so elegant!

6. For a really glamorous look, add a strand of pearls around Hello Kitty's neck. Gorgeous!

Nature Girl

Now that school's out, Hello Kitty has lots of free time. Lace up your hiking boots and join her on a nature hike!

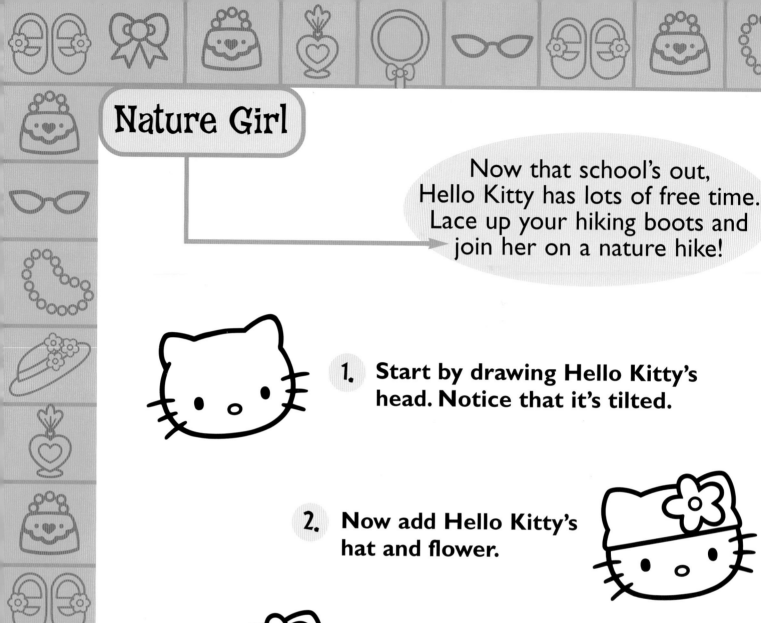

1. **Start by drawing Hello Kitty's head. Notice that it's tilted.**

2. **Now add Hello Kitty's hat and flower.**

3. **Next, draw the top of Hello Kitty's body.**

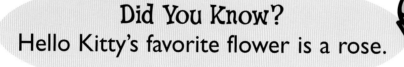
Did You Know?
Hello Kitty's favorite flower is a rose.

4. Now draw Hello Kitty's sneaker and pants. Add treads to the bottom of her sneaker.

Hello Kitty looks like she's walking because her feet are in different positions. Make sure to include this in your drawing.

5. Add Hello Kitty's other sneaker. Make sure it's laced up!

6. There are lots of birds for Hello Kitty to see. Give her a pair of binoculars so she's sure not to miss them!

Beach Fun

Hello Kitty loves spending warm summer days at the beach. And what's better than a game of beach volleyball?

1. **Start by drawing Hello Kitty's head. She's wearing a special flower!**

2. **Now draw Hello Kitty's tank top.**

3. **Add Hello Kitty's arms.**

Did You Know?
Hello Kitty plants a tomato garden every summer.

4. Draw Hello Kitty's bathing suit bottom and her legs, too.

Since this is a summer scene, color your drawing with warm colors like red, orange, and yellow.

5. Hello Kitty loves her flip-flops! Can you draw them?

6. Now draw a volleyball under Hello Kitty's arm. She's ready to serve!

7. Hello Kitty won't let the sun ruin her game! Draw a visor on her head to keep the sun out of her eyes.

Whether she's at a school dance or cheering her team to victory, Hello Kitty's style is all her own. And thanks to you, Hello Kitty has never looked better!

Remember—the more you practice, the better your drawings will be. Once you've mastered the drawings in this book, why not create some fashion designs of your own? With Hello Kitty as a model, you'll be dressing pretty in any outfit!